IF I AM POETRY, THEN YOU ARE MY WORDS

आयुषी जदिल

Made with ♥ on the Notion Press Platform
www.notionpress.com

Contents

1. How Are Some Relationships Made? 1
2. What Is Love? 3
3. Love Is Not Just Words 4
4. Letter To The Love 5
5. Thread Of Love 6
6. Tell Me What Should I Write Today...! 7
7. It's Him 8
8. Waiting For Someone Without Hope Is Love 9
9. Two Step 10
10. You Have To Write Your Last Wish...! 11
11. Complete My Love To Convince 12
12. Expressing Love 13
13. How Do I Love Thee? 14
14. One Day 16
15. I Need To Confide To The Love Of My Life 17
16. I Want To Be With You 19
17. I Never Want To Stop Making Memories With You. 21
18. I Want You 22
19. Often In Love 23
20. I Don't Want... 24
21. I Have Trusted 25
22. Your My Relationship 26
23. Blank Paper Of My Heart 27
24. I Wish 28

Contents

25. You Are My Life 29

26. Love Letter To My Special Human 30

27. He's Mine 32

28. Untagged Bond 33

29. A Wish 34

30. 35

31. A Forever 36

32. My Love In 90's 37

33. Loving You 38

34. You're Important To Me 40

35. Him 41

36. This Relationship Of Love 42

37. Whenever You Live... 43

38. Dedicated To You 44

39. A Moment With You 45

40. You're Special! 46

41. Yeah He's Messy! (i Never Imagined My Love To Be Perfect) 47

42. Will You Marry Me? 49

It's All About Love 51

1. How are some relationships made?

How are some relationships made?
It is not known.
When, who, how and
where he comes close to us,
everything happens so quickly, we
cannot even think about anything.
It dominates our thinking.
Heart wants to just keep looking at him.
The bells kept talking.
They get nervous when there is
no talk There is a strange
happiness every moment. Get him without
meeting him. It is good
to wait, eager to tell everything. Looking
for an excuse to talk. Sometimes
resentment is also expressed.
It becomes like a right on that.
Afraid of losing It
becomes necessary instead of being necessary.
And it becomes necessary.
Thinking about him If only!
Would have got it earlier.

They even shed tears for him.
Start living in a different world.
Where there is only and only love and love.

2. What is love?

What is love?
It is a binding
Where never lets you go.
What is love?
It is a cut
Which bleeds your mortal soul.
What is love?
It is a joy
Which comes from sharing your life with another.
What is love?
It is two people
Which are one.

3. Love is not just words

This is the feeling
that turns a stone into gold, this
is delicate like dew and
Whomever you touch, touch
him, unite him with God.
This is the river in which
if someone drowns cross it
this is the happiness,
In front of which everything
in the world looks pale
this is the pain that
Let the sea merge in your
eyelids, love is very simple
But his statement...
very difficult...!

4. Letter to the LOVE

I won't hesitate this time,
No signs, no clues.
My words will be clear
as crystal sky blue.
I know this sounds crazy as 90's love,
And it probably is,
because I love you, and it's Undeniable truth.
What I've been see in you,
It's pure as brand new.
You're the blood that flow
through my veins and the
Heart that beats inside my chest.
These words are not enough
to express how virtuous you are!
Yes/no, sleep on it, beautiful.
I'm ready to accept slap and
Standing right behind your back,
Opening my arms.

5. Thread of love

We are connected by the thread of
love, This bond is of birth, It is
connected with a raw thread, But
this bond of true thread was
written somewhere in the sky,
This meeting happened on earth.
I met a stranger for a
day, but we are strangers,
life is without you, you are
the reason for my laughter.
We share the pain with happiness,
no matter how we spend time, whether
we are far away or near, we
sort out the moments with happiness.
I pray that in this moment of
meeting, you stay in me, I stay in you,
this world is small and fragrant,
flowers keep blooming in this gulshan.

6. Tell me what should I write today...!

Think a little, then write one thing,
write feelings or write situations,
Should I write your love with me,
or should I write your hand in my hands,
After seeing you, should I write about you,
should I write praise or should I write complaint,
Should I write myself inhabited behind you, or
should I write myself ruined in loneliness,
Should I write you day or myself night, tell
me which thing should I write today...!

7. It's him

It's him who made me fall in love with surprises,
Coz that's how destiny brought us together,
It's him who has become my habit,
Coz I'm wearing the smile he has given me.
It's him who stole my heart,
Coz it's me who stole his sight,
It's him who's not perfect for everyone,
Coz he's flawless in a world that's mine.
It's him; the one I crave for,
Coz he's my best; not favourite,
It's him where my world begins,
Coz it's him where it will end.
"You are sunlight through a window, which
I stand in' warmed. My darling."

8. Waiting for someone without hope is love

When did you understand love?
Who will explain to me.
In your words.
Will you bother me now?
I know what is the meaning of love.
What new definition will you tell me?
Attachment to anyone is not love.
To have attachment without seeing someone is love.
What kind of love is it to be happy after meeting someone.
Keeping someone as a wish is love.
To talk to someone is love,
in front of someone.
To forget everything is love.
How is love to get someone?
To be desperate for someone is love.
Shedding tears for someone is not love.
To smile for someone is love.
Waiting for someone without hope is love.

9. Two step

You walk two steps, we walk two steps.
Let's complete the distance like this.
Life has been found for four days here.
Is it our place or your place. Staying away is
just helplessness dear. Where will you
get time to come near? Those who fall
are yours, those who fall are us. Forgetting
everything, start a new series. You
walk two steps, we walk two steps. Let's
complete the distance like this.
No one could stand the path of time.
Some went on, some could not walk.
The one who walked and walked,
went. The one who stopped there got lost
on the way. I hold you, you hold me
Decide to travel life together. You walk
two steps, we walk two steps. Let's
complete the distance like this.

10. You have to write your last wish...!

Today I have to write something lovely,
I have to write you on the blank paper of my heart,
I do not know the claims of love,
I just want to write your name to myself,
My lips yearn for a smile, I am
happy with you, I have to write this,
I love you very deeply, you
have to write your last wish...!

11. Complete my love to convince

In one birth, waited for a hundred births
Complete my love To convince you,
To show love, How many faces have been made,
Waking up all night and singing love requests
from a free heart, Surrender from the heart, Accept
complete my love to convince you.
Should I say Gul, should I say Gulshan or should
I say spring, when you smile, it is like waterfalls
My body and mind remained fragrant, make
the world complete my love
Ishq Dariya, Josh Kashti, what should you think of
the consequences Radha and Ghanshyam have been sung for
ages, take care of my boat, become the rudder
complete my love to convince you.

12. Expressing love

Everyone has their own
rules for expressing love.
Shah Jahan built the magnificent
Taj Mahal in memory of his Mumtaz.
In the desire of his Laila, Majnun
tolerated even the stones of the world with a smile.
I see the light in her eyes,
kiss her soft hands,
I settle in his arms.

13. How do I love thee?

How do I love thee? Let me count the ways.
You won't find this on any public displays
But when you look into my eyes
It glows in bold so don't be surprised
I think of you in the morning
As I awake from sleep
Looking at the first light of the sun ray
I wish you have a fruitful day
As I close my eyes deep in meditation
My thoughts go wandering
When will I see you again
This distance becoming an enduring pain
I can hear your voice, deep, soft, and slow in my head
Words of everlasting love
creating feelings that are
impossible to express
You make me forget that
I was ever bruised or broken,
my wings feel light and free
The kindness in your smile
puts all my doubts to sleep.
The need to touch you, to feel you, to drink you in
is almost too much to hold

Thanking my lucky stars for this gift
of love pure and gold
Those moments we snatch from time
And you soak me, in your passionate bliss
I want to make that time stand still
And drown in your endless kiss
I think of you when the rays of moonlight
spill like a waterfall between the blinds
and settle somewhere
in my dreamy eyes.
This feeling I have, I wish I could freeze.
It's deep within and makes me shake at the knees
It's my love for you that keeps going strong,
This love now lives permanently in my soul

14. One day

I want to walk a long with you in the night
I want your hand in my hand as couples
I want you to be with me in the morning on the bed
I want to kiss you on forehead whenever you got scare
I want to huge you to stop crying for me
I want to tell the world how much I love you
I want you to be my heaven forever
I want to propose you in my bestest way
I want to make you smile when, you don't even want to
I want to correct all your mistakes, by just holding your hand
I want to say don't scare I'm here, whenever you need to
listen it
#But
This one day can't complete, if you were not with me
please be mine my life, I love you

15. I need to confide to the love of my life

I need to confide,
True love is hard to find,
But I found someone,
on whom I can rely my whole life!
Finally I found you,
After searching you For an Eternity!
We were meant to be together,
Yes, that's the destiny!
I gave you all my ecstasy,
The thought of you was heavenly,
We are strong together,
If seperated, then we'll die!
Somewhere in Myself,
I am scared of my own demise!
Eyes, on you forever!
Will be there for you FOREVER AND EVER!
In my dark phase,
Just in case, You will be my light!
That shiny bright light,
Who will take me from the dark!
I don't know how much I love you,
I don't know how much I care about you!

I don't know how much I want you!
But all that I know is that I finally found you!!!

16. I want to be with you

Hey handsome,
How are you,
Let me tell you,
I love you.
You are the best thing happened to me,
Let's leave the fate on whatever it will be,
Let's enjoy our time,
I am yours and you are mine.
Love is not about touch,
It's about the feeling,
You have all the rights even to say shush,
I got this feeling, that we will be better together.
I don't have words to describe you,
You are different from others, you are just you.
Yea, yea I know have made a few mistakes before,
But I am a better person now, (let's go on a sea shore)
I like me better when I am with you,
I like you more than any can,
Once again my love, I love you
I will be nothing without you.
Let's support each other on this journey together,
No if, may but or whatever.
I love you like my poems,

I want to be with you.

17. I never want to stop making memories with you.

I may not be the easiest
person to love.
I might have trust issue at first.
But I just want you to know
one important thing about me;
If I date, I date to marry.
If I decide to spend time with you,
it's because see potential in you.
I'm not here to lose time or
just have some fun.
If I'm with you, it's because
I see my future in you.
It's not gonna be easy,
I know that.
But it's defiantly gonna worth it.
I promise.

18. I want you

I want you everyday
Even when you're mad, at me
when you irritate me and when you piss me off
I want you gram I want your happy days and you
I don't want to be alive even a single day
I want you in the early mornings and
in middle of the dark nights
I want to be the only reason
behind your sweet smile
And loudlaughters everyday
Even when you are sad
I want to kiss you and to be in your arms
I want to hold you and to stay up all night talking
I want to fell for you and
to protect you from all
the things in the world

19. Often in love

Some insolence is justified
If someone wants
It is justified to keep wishing someone for a long time.
To die on someone
It is justified to live after seeing someone.
Getting angry with someone
So it is justified to celebrate someone
To express to someone
So somewhere silence is justified.
Smiling at someone
It is permissible to see someone smiling.
To think of someone
It is justified to be destroyed in someone.
Worrying about someone
So it is permissible to pray for someone.
To make someone yours
it is permissible for someone to forget himself.

20. I don't want...

I don’t want a promise with you,
I want the promise of your love.
I don’t want a promise to meet you,
I want a promise to remember.
I don’t want promises of daily talks,
I need a promise to listen to me.
I don’t promise to laugh together,
I need a promise to wipe the tears.
I don’t want the promise of dreams,
I want the promise of reality.
I don’t want the promise of your time,
I want a promise of your feeling

21. I have trusted

You more than my life.
Tell me after thinking.
What is your intention now?
Holding your arm, I will
cross the river of love.
I don't care
anymore Somehow
You are my life
You are my love now.
Know now you too, This
poor heart should never break.
With great difficulty, I
have learned to smile again.

22. Your my relationship

Your my relationship
Beyond all relationships
Which is not possible to tie in any circle.
Nor can anyone give its definition.
Such a relationship
The one who makes the impossible possible,
increases the possibilities,
like a ray of hope in life.
Sorry for that
Which is not visible.
But it does exist.
It is present everywhere one particle.
Like that tree.
Whic also holds dry twigs, like a firefly.
Illuminates that plant.
With whom he is closely related.
Like that dew drop.
The leaf on which it falls.
It gets merged in that.

23. Blank paper of my heart

Today I have to write something lovely,
I have to write you on the blank paper of my heart,
I do not know the claims of love,
I just want to write your name to myself,
My lips yearn for a smile, I am happy
with you, I have to write this,
I love you very deeply, you
have to write your last wish...!

24. I wish

Be face to face with you...
I wish to hear something,
get lost in your words...
I wish to lose my pain,
Drowned in your love...
I wish to forget myself,
Keep my head in your lap...
I wish to sleep carefree,
Now sitting in prostration to God...
I have a desire to ask you...
that for a few moments now...
I have a desire to stay in your shelters,
That now I should be face to face with you...
I have the desire to get lost in you..!!

25. You are my life

I found you even in the crowd
I found you even in loneliness,
When I am with people, then you are near me,
when I am alone, then you hold my hand,
I do not understand, is this the story of
your love or the scene of my love,
I have only understood that,
you are in my happiness, my sorrows
I am in you, you are in my life,
you are in every moment of my life

26. Love letter to my special human

A letter to you, to unfold our journey of togetherness.
To the man I love, here I say this.
Falling in love with you has created a
stronger and sustained connect to my soul.
In this world while technology is been dominating,
I still sit down with my paper and pen,
to pen down my emotions and feelings.
As I don't want them to influence
and consume my love for you.
When the sun rises,
my heart feels the pleasure of joy,
I think about you, and your eyes.
Which is warm and bright looking at me.
Your fingers caress me quietly to hold my
hands tight,
making me feel so safe within.
Your arms pull me closer in the middle of
the night as you know my mind seek you
even at that time.
I never had to stutter while choosing words
to convey it to you,
as your hug understands it,

to wrap me with a forehead kiss.
You are my strong pillar of happiness,
compassion and a shelter of peace.
Saving these tiny pieces of letters
every time I write. So I can gather one day
and give it to you.
I am fortunate to have found a man who is
filled with commitment, loyalty
and magic in making a life together.
You make me feel exceptional
every single day.
My heart always belongs to You even in these
love letters.
Yours,
_aayushi jindal

27. He's MINE

I love him like no one else does
I'm not his mother but won't be much
He's got the face of an angel
But the smile says he's evil
Fair so bright the sun won't shine
Holds me tight until I'm crying
Looks at me like he's lucky alive
To be with me but that's not fine
I've been with people worse and worse
He's been the best and its not a verse
I know I say it every time
But this time I'll prove it that he'll stay mine

28. Untagged bond

The things that is between us is beyond words.
You make me realise what really "SUKOON" means.
Everything between us is magical,
the way you understands my eyes,
the way you encourages me,
the way you always there for me whenever I needed.
I always found the real version of me with you, i.e;
with no filters,no bolne se phle sochna, no fearing of judging.
I speak my heart out in front of you.
We found a corner in each other's life
where we feel like we can together rock the world
our laughter, our fights,our wrangling is
something which makes us more confident about each other.
We never put a tag on our relation,
because that tag will never justify
how much we mean for each other.
This world..!! Ahemm...
have so much to talk about us,
have so much to let us down and judge,
they put allegations, but the only thing.
I care about is what you think about me, and
I know you will always understand me like you always did..!!

29. A wish

Let's go out in the cold of winter
Talking on the road late at night
You stop and come in front of me
Your eyes point totally my eyesight
Time seems to be stopped,
A pleasant cold like love, can be felt
You hug me and feel the warmth
I hold you tight and tight, lets melt
Your name, my belief and my faith
If your heart beats, I take breath
Your pain, my muff my weakness
Your love, my energy my strength
We seem to have come a long way
Time passed quickly, you also look tired
Let's take this plesent walk to home
Come sit on my back and enjoy the ride

30.

Before I met you.
I didn't know if love existed
And then you came and showed me
what is love.
I found my true love in you.
The way you make me feel
is different in every way.
The happiness you give me
is that no can give.
Your gentle hug always melt me
Your tender words comfort me
I crave for your presence now..!!
You are my home.
I want you.
Nothing else, Just you.

31. A forever

Will you still love me when I get old?
Will you feel the same as today?
And feel pleased in every little way? Will you try and make me laugh?
Will you talk over calls and chat with me daily? Will you still be cuddling the same way?
And feel proud when you seek me in the bathtub? Will you still make bed time tea for me?
Will you still tell me I am beautiful inside out?
And take care of me?
Will you always hold me in your arms?
Will you still make me safe?
Will you still will get to know what I am thinking?
Just by reading my eye's reflecting everything on my face?
And if you want to go with this ahead?
Then there is our sweet life together
So, you need to say yes to all the statements and questions
Then, I am sure this will last FOREVER.

32. My love in 90's

My love would be different,
It wouldn't have been on rent.
I would have loved you more,
No matter even if our love you tore.
If I had loved you in 90s,
I would have have danced
with you on streets.
Just like Geet with Aditya did,
I will be forever kid.
My love will be for you and only you,
From your life I will remove the blues.
You're mine and I will yours,
That's a secret untold.

33. Loving you

My love, this gloom doesn't really suit your face
I'll feel blessed to take you out, of this state
Let your dry lips be wet as I brush them with mine
Let your eyes, be closed while I make you experience the divine
I'll soak up all your worries I promise
And will probably leave you, blushing after we kiss
I know times are tough for you darlin'
That roads are steep and curved simultaneously
Things aren't as nice as always
Neither are they always easy
But I would love to to pluck all thorns lying on your way
Puneet, just promise me less of dismay
I'm ready with my heart open to exchange all your doldrums
With my peace and happiness
For my happiness without you is a mess
I'm often not vocal, of my feelings for you
But trust me, my love, my heart doesn't wanna see you in gloomy rage
I have waited for us to be true for years
That my eyes and heart are simultaneously shedding tears
To be blessed with you and not your thoughts for the very time, tonight first

Come on, place your tired head on my beating heart, hold my hands,tight
Let's kiss under the light of a thousand stars
I can't just tell you, how happy i'm for here we are
You have made me smile like I never cried
You always do that for me
And I win every battle i'm facing
Wonder how great of a magic are you?
That you make me, believe of things, I never thought to
Love was one of them
And since i've found you I've known no gem
Like you and loving.

34. You're important to me

You're important to me.
To my bones and body
Like my own soul
Once had been
I would keep you
In my eyes and scented sweaters
And in pictures turning yellow in my purse
I pass by thousands of them everyday
No one lingers longer on my way
But you my love linger all over me
All the time and even Sundays
Ik what actually is the case
Perhaps multiverse is real of a thing
And I wanna love you in every Verse like I'm doing
And sing To you at 2AM
"Tujhse o deewane, kbhi mohabbat na maine krni thi,
magar mere dil ne mujhe dhokha de diya."

35. Him

He is the one,
I used to craft within my dreams,
That one fine soul,
I always had wanted to share myself with,
Who is undoubtedly an attention seeker,
Yes! My little attention is utmost precious to him,
Whose not so heavy pocket is enough to give pretty joys to me,
He is childish,
He is cute,
He has it all I wished him to be,
My man is just perfect,
And I love to be possessive for him,
Yes I frown,
I don't want anyone to use him even behind pronouns !

36. This relationship of love

The one who is the most beloved
in this world, like this whole world,
our relationship is just like that,
This relationship is of love,
This is a relation of trust,
this is a relation of emotions,
and of many beautiful meetings,
which started with quarrels,
will never end now.
Staying together, celebrating,
and not hiding anything from each other,
a lot of love is hidden even in anger,
that's why we forget our mistakes every time,
Let's stay together like this only,
there should never be any dispute.

37. Whenever you live...

Wherever you live,
you will definitely meet us,
"Wherever we meet...
If we don't meet then in the world...!"
"If you live in your life...
If you don't live in your body....!! "
From where till life...
the sky has been the earth,
in the same way you will always be mine....!!

38. Dedicated to you

You are a sharp
edged sword.
Irreparable
it's a sweet hit.
My heart
is my life.
My ego
is my pride.
Beautiful graceful
eyes intoxicating.
Soft cheeks and
juicy lips.
Day with you
night with you.
Knows your
eye communication.
You are my pride.
You are my life.
You are my happiness,
You are my smile.

39. A moment with you

Let me spend a moment with you,
never leave your hand.
Never end such a night,
where you and I are together.
It just rains, our love keeps growing,
there should never be any dispute between us.
When you get angry, convince me friend.
Love should never end,
today I express to you,
accept it now my dear.
Let me spend a moment with you,
hand in hand, talk about love to each other,
our relationship should be like this for seven births.
Tell each other whatever you want to say,
don't stay away from each other anymore.
Then see how beautiful this weather looks,
how colorful this world looks with you.

40. You're special!

You don't have to ask,
If you're special,
For I talk about you most of the time,
And hold your memories,
Within my lovely rhymes,
I care for you too but that I feel shy to admit,
I fear if I might not be the one you plan your life with,
I admire you in countless ways,
I sit by your pictures,
I smile as I gaze,
And you don't have to make me feel special too,
Sending thousand hearts,
Your single honest emotion,
Is absolutely enough to melt my heart.

41. Yeah he's messy! (I never imagined my love to be perfect)

I never wanted him to be perfect!
In fact my love for him is even messier than
he is and the best part is that beauty lies in imperfections.
Though he is insane yet a masterpiece and
for me a perfect person to fall in love with.
He is my lovely shade of crazy and
yes I have fallen for his bizarre care and
for me he and his love, both are impeccable.
His untarnished warmth has touched my cold soul!
His way of endearment has made me lovesick.
His sweet talks have landed me in an aura of love...pure love!
The synonyms he uses for me, each day,
make me feel and believe his unending, eternal love,
which is whispered by his breath every second,
and is inculcated in his eyes forever and ever.
His words are just a bridge between his feelings and my heart!
He is the one whose soul is so pure.
He is the one who has proved to be an angel for me!
He is the best gift I have found!

He is my happiness, my smile,my laugh, and much much more!
And yes I love him!!!

42. Will you marry me?

Hey! You
Wanna say this now...
You so cute today,
Ever seen like you!
Wanna hold your hand...
Just make a tight hug
With a lots of love!
Try to see both eyes and share our love!
The lips are try to fight.
The fingers are ready to mingle!
Even the hands are redy to hold you...
The heat says! I love you my love!
Finally I forget all when I see your eyes.
Am surrender when I show you...
The angel of my world...
Will you marry me?

It's All About Love

Love is not only about having meet ups and
spending lots of time together but I think that
love is all about that force which not only
keeps us together when we are alive but also
keeps us together even after death..
Because Log chale jaate hain Pyaar hardum saath hi rehta
hai....

9 798889 758679

Printed by Libri Plureos GmbH in Hamburg, Germany